A Note to Parents

Rhyme, Repetition, and Reading are 3 R's that make learning fun for your child. **Rhyme Time Readers** will introduce your child to the sounds of language, providing the foundation for reading success.

Rhyme

Children learn to listen and to speak before they learn to read. When you read this book, you are helping your child connect spoken language to written language. This increased awareness of sound helps your child with phonics and other important reading skills. While reading this book, encourage your child to identify the rhyming words on each page.

Repetition

Rhyme Time Readers have stories that your child will ask you to read over and over again. The words will become memorable due to frequent readings. To keep it fresh, take turns reading, and encourage your child to chime in on the rhyming words.

Reading

Someday your child will be reading this book to you, as learning sounds leads to reading words and finally to reading stories like this one. I hope this book makes reading together a special experience.

Have fun and take the time to let your child read and rhyme.

Francie Alexander

—Chief Education Officer,
Scholastic's Learning Ventures

For Steven, Casey, and Rachel—
my "ice cream kids"
—M.B.P.

To Josh and Ellie, ice cream experts
—S.R.

ISBN: 0-439-33397-0

Text copyright © 2002 by Marjorie Blain Parker.
Illustrations copyright © 2002 by Stephanie Roth.
All rights reserved. Published by Scholastic Inc.
SCHOLASTIC, RHYME TIME READERS, CARTWHEEL BOOKS,
and associated logos are trademarks and/or registered trademarks of Scholastic Inc.

Library of Congress Cataloging-in-Publication Data
Parker, Marjorie Blain.
    Ice cream everywhere!/ by Marjorie Blain Parker; illustrated by Stephanie Roth.
        p. cm.— (Rhyme time readers)
    Summary: Rhyming text describes different ways of eating ice cream and how to clean up afterwards.
        ISBN 0-439-33397-0
    [1. Ice cream, ices, etc.—Fiction. 2. Stories in rhyme.] I. Roth, Stephanie, ill.
II. Title. III. Series.
PZ8.P17 Ic 2002
[E]—dc21   2001040020

30 29 28 27 26 25 24 23 22   14/0

Printed in the U.S.A. 40
First printing, May 2002

Ice Cream Everywhere!

by Marjorie Blain Parker
Illustrated by Stephanie Roth

SCHOLASTIC INC. Cartwheel BOOKS®

New York   Toronto   London   Auckland   Sydney
Mexico City   New Delhi   Hong Kong   Buenos Aires

I scream.
You scream.

We all scream for ice cream!

Ice cream in a cone.

Ice cream in a cup.

Ice cream all alone.

Ice cream all fixed up.

Ice cream in a float.

Ice cream and some cake.

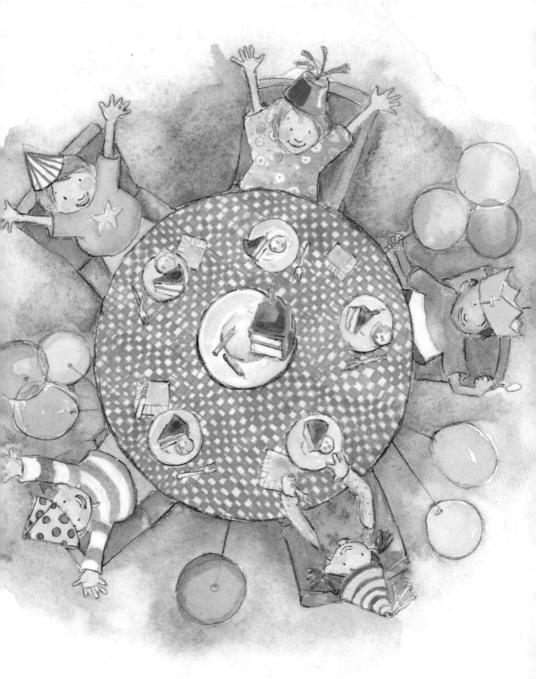

Ice cream in a boat.

Ice cream in a shake.

Drip. Lick.

Ice cream stick.

Stir. Scoop.

Ice cream soup.

Gulp. Slurp.

Ice cream burp!

Ice cream

on your face.

Ice cream

in your hair.

Ice cream

everyplace.

Ice cream

everywhere.

Scrub. Wash.
Spill and slosh.

Mess. Stain.
Down the drain.

I scream.
You scream.
We all scream for ice cream!